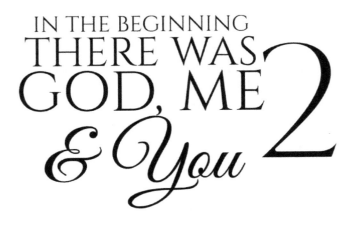

IN THE BEGINNING THERE WAS GOD, ME & You 2

A JOURNEY INTO A TRUE CHRISTIAN ROMANCE

ANGIE BEE & BARTEE

Reading for the Whole Person

INSPIRED published by

Ladero Press LLC

229 Kettering Road

Deltona, Florida 32725

First Ladero Press Printing, April 2021

In the Beginning: There Was God, Me & You 2

Copyright © 2021 by Angela Neal and Eugene Neal

Contributions from members of *The TOUR that Angie BEE Presents*

All rights reserved.

ISBN: 978-1-946981-78-3 Paperback / 978-1-946981-79-0 EPUB 978-1-946981-80-6 MOBI

Printed in the United States of America

Set in Palatino Quattrocento Sans and Cinzel Regular

Cover Designed by SheerGenius

Edited by Spirit of Excellence Writing & Editing Services, LLC

Cover Photo Credits: Jhonn De La Puente

Scripture quotations are taken from the Holy Bible, New Living Translation, Copyright ©1996, 2004, 2007, 2013, 2015 by Tyndale House Foundation. Used by permission of Tyndale House Publishers, Inc., Carol Stream, Illinois 60188. All rights reserved.

Scripture quotations are from the ESV® Bible (The Holy Bible, English Standard Version®), copyright © 2001 by Crossway, a publishing ministry of Good News Publishers. Used by permission. All rights reserved.

Scripture quotations marked (NIV) are taken from the Holy Bible, New International Version®, NIV®. Copyright © 1973, 1978, 1984, 2011 by Biblica, Inc.™ Used by permission of Zondervan. All rights reserved worldwide. www.zondervan.comThe "NIV" and "New International Version" are trademarks registered in the United States Patent and Trademark Office by Biblica, Inc.™

All rights reserved. The reproduction, transmission, or utilization of this work in whole or in part in any form by any electronic, mechanical or other means, now known or hereafter invented, including xerography, photocopying and recording, or in any information storage or retrieval system, is forbidden without written permission. For permission, please contact *Ladero Press Editors at* editors@laderopress.com.

The INSPIRED logo is a trademark of Ladero Press.

The *Where Writers Can Soar* logo is a trademark of Ladero Press.

Library of Congress information available upon request.

www.laderopress.com

www.DaQueenBee.com

TABLE OF CONTENTS

THOUGHTS FROM A FEW FRIENDS ON THE JOURNEY

❧

This Joker Told Me He Didn't Know Her

*A*ngie BEE and Bartee ... *Sound good together! They would look really good together; I wonder if he knows her? I should mention her to him. Nah, I should mind my own business.* So, I did just that. I minded my own business. But every time I would look at Bartee, I would wonder the same things repeatedly. *Does he know her? Have they at least met each other? And if they have met, why are they not together?* I'm no matchmaker. I have never played matchmaker a day in my life. But my Spirit is calling on me to at least ask him about her. I cannot seem to let it go.

But ... I don't even really know Angie BEE. She's my Facebook friend. I know Bartee well. We have worked together for a couple of years. I know that he is single.

He is a solid dude. I believe Angie BEE is a solid God-loving female. I like her. I like the spirit that radiates from her Facebook page. I know enough about her to know that he would like her, too. He needs somebody, and she seems like that somebody that he needs. I don't know. Maybe she's already with someone? But if she is with someone, why does she pop into my mind every time I look at Bartee?

Months later, here I am at work talking to Bartee. He's standing at my desk chitchatting and before I can stop myself, I just blurt it out. "Do you know Angie BEE?" Bartee replies, "No, who is that?" I say, "I think she's a promoter in the area. She does some type of media work." Bartee says he has never met her. I go silent and think, *That's too bad.* We continue to talk about everything except what was really on my mind--the lingering question—*why don't you know Angie BEE?* I never mention her to him again.

A few months later, Angie BEE walks into our workplace with none other than Bartee!!! Wait, what the ... This joker told me he didn't know her. As soon as I see her, I yell, "Angie BEE!" She smiles and walks over toward my desk. I introduce myself quickly. I tell her that we're Facebook friends. He shows her around a little bit. She looks at the office space. They say good-bye and leave.

Not long after that, they're married. Now, I know the Lord works in mysterious ways, and we may never know all the inner most workings of God, but this is mind-blowing to me. And I am smiling from ear to ear because what's meant to be will be. God's plan is unchangeable, and no one in the universe can stop that. The vision that God has for our lives will happen, as He has already purposed it. His purpose will always stand. He will do all that He pleases.

Lafreida Gallon

Lafreida Gallon is a Court Services Manager for the Seventh Judicial Circuit Court of Florida. Her passion is to see people continually do better, no matter where the motivation to do so comes from. Lafreida lives on the East Coast of Florida with her husband Michael Gallon. She has three boys and one girl ranging in ages from 18 to 27.

Email: GodlyMedicine@outlook.com

AND THAT, MY FRIEND, IS LOVE

～

I was invited to ride along with Angie BEE & Bartee so on this particular day I was at their home. This was one of my earliest experiences traveling with *The TOUR that Angie BEE Presents*. Angie BEE had packed everything she needed, and we were waiting on Bartee to arrive. I had never seen inside the garage before but when I did, B-A-B-Y... it was tight up in there. Every available space was taken. Bartee patiently pulled out everything they needed like tables, tents, speakers, a sound system, chairs, etc., and he methodically packed it in the vehicle along with the things Angie BEE had in the house. I don't know how he did it, but it all fit in the SUV ... including me. I only had to hold my purse, a basket of door prizes, and a case of water on my lap.

Bartee, the Rage of the Stage, completed this task going and coming home with a little sweat on his brow and love in his heart.

Have you seen commercials where a couple appears to be blissfully happy and content with each other – smiling, laughing, touching, and kissing, like two birds sitting in a tree? This is the image I have of Bartee and Angie BEE. Since the day I met them, they exude the joy of the Lord. It is not because their relationship is perfect … it is because they seek the Lord from whence cometh their help. God helps them see the good when things are not so good. I consider it pure JOY and a blessing whenever I'm with them … and that my friend is LOVE.

Loretha Q. Simon – Recent graduate of International Seminary, Diploma of Practical Theology, Restoration Church of Daytona, Inc. #LoveDaytonaBeach

- Loretha Simon

A WORD FROM MR. CHARLES PARKER

E ugene Bartee, my brother from another mother. I met Eugene back in the 70s through his brother William Bartee. I played bass guitar and sang backup vocals. Bartee and I really got to know each other after William passed away. We started singing together as a group along with two other vocalists.

We performed for many occasions. I moved from DeLand, Florida, to Atlanta, Georgia, in 1988 to pursue a job career in law enforcement. Bartee and I slowed down performing together but didn't stop. Over the years Bartee has enhanced his talent, good stage presence, and very good showmanship. I really enjoy watching him perform! I am proud of you, my Brother.

Angie really changed Bartee in a very good way. She taught him how to promote, and she showed him what we should stand for. She even taught me about promotion! Thank you.

As of today, Bartee and I are members of the group Meta IV, singing old-school R&B, funk, pop & gospel. We aim to please!

WE GO BACK
WE GO WAY BACK!

—～〜—

I really didn't want to get into a personal blow-by-blow of our times together, but I will start by saying that I met Bartee back in 1973. My Higher Power has placed many people in my life who have influenced me and changed my life. I met Bartee in 1973 while being incarcerated at Mansfield Reformatory. They say that true friendship is someone who has your back, no matter what! They watch out for you and ensure you are not in danger. They will NEVER purposely lead you into making bad decisions, that aren't good for you. A true friend like Bartee will always have your best interest at heart.

He has always been loyal and dependable by staying in touch and by seeing if I am doing all right. Even though he is only a couple of years younger than me, I consider him my younger brother. I am very grateful and blessed to have him in my life. There are a whole lot of things that we have done in our lives; we were even roommates for a while after we were incarcerated. I just wanted to take this time to share what his friendship means to me.

Since marrying Angie BEE, I think he found someone that he can really bond with. I think the two of them are really "into each other" because they do things together, and they even do a show on Facebook together. I think he finally found someone that he truly loves. HAPPY WIFE, HAPPY LIFE! Thank you, Bartee.

By Walter "Tiki" Blount aka "Teek-Dog"

Photo Credit by Angie BEE

Summer 2020

ACKNOWLEDGEMENTS

O ur God is a wonder! He brought us together, and then navigated us over the bumps in the road. Lord, thank you for the trials, the tribulations, and the romance. We aren't the perfect couple, *but our love for you is as perfect as can be*. We give you all the praise, and we thank you for continuing our true love story.

- Angie BEE & Bartee

CHAPTER 1
ONE BLANKET FOR
THE TWO OF US!

It was a Saturday morning, and the temperature outside had dropped overnight. The space heater was on when we drifted off to sleep the night before, but somewhere around midnight, it had become too hot in the room, so I had turned it off. Now the sun was rising, and the shivering began.

"Please pass me some blanket, Honey," I whispered in my husband's ear. He was sprawled on top of the blanket, snoring peacefully, and I hated to wake him up, but I was cold! What was my husband's response to my question? "Come on over here, baby. I got one blanket for the two of us."

As I cuddled up next to my husband and even up-and-over to my joyous place on top of him, my mind became delighted by his statement! When does "the loving" begin? When the music starts playing? When the kissing begins, or when you submit to God and His plans for your lives together?! One Faith, One God, One Baptism, One Blanket.

The Bible tells us that two people can't walk in the same direction unless they agree. When do we paint the house? We must agree on the color and the budget. When do we go on vacation? We must agree on the same days off and the destination. When shall we make love? Mornings, evenings or "afternoon delights"? We two must agree to serve the Lord with gladness TOGETHER – one blanket for the two of us.

Do two walk together unless they have agreed to do so? Amos 3:3 NLT

Bartee's Response

First of all, we have three blankets on the bed! My wife starts with all three. We have a big ceiling fan, which she prefers to have the setting on HIGH. For me, it's already too hot in the room, winter OR summer, and so I have to leave one leg uncovered – sometimes, before I take ALL of the cover off of me, in order to get comfortable. At this particular time, I had one blanket on and the other two thrown back; my wife was covered in all three! Then, I heard a voice say, "Please pass me some blanket, Honey." You already know what I replied.

NOW! Knowing that my wife likes to cuddle up every night, in my arms, I just thought it was one of those "love-making" suggestions.   And the rest (as they say) is history!

Photo credit by

Lesley Reed

CHAPTER 2
YOUR BELLY MAY BE FAT, BUT YOUR BOTTOM IS PERFECT!

There are times when individuals must compromise as they begin a relationship. If you want to have people in your life and you want those relationships to last, you need to learn to compromise.

For example, I am a girly-girl. I LOVE to wear dresses! I don't enjoy wearing pants, and I REALLY despise denim. My maternal granddad grew up in Macon, Georgia, in the 1920s and 1930s, and he really didn't like wearing blue jeans. Granddaddy used to say, "Blue jeans is all a poor nigga could wear when I was a kid, so I don't ever want to see MY kids wearing them!" My mom never allowed us to wear denim when she took us to see our grandparents, and I continued to carry that lesson through to my adult life. I don't like blue jeans!

What is it about men and their fascination with blue jeans? I knew a brother in college that LOVED his women to wear blue jeans and high-heeled shoes! I don't know, but I wasn't compromising back then! Hmmph. Well, Bartee likes blue jeans. He loves to wear them, work in them, play in them, and rehearse in them. Well, that's for him ... that ain't for me. (Heavy sigh.)

"Honey! I bought you some blue jeans!" my husband exclaimed with excitement while entering our home one day. I really had to check my response because when my head snatched around in his direction, I almost cussed. "What did you say, dear?" was my response. "I found these blue jeans in your size and I think you will look great in them!" he said through his wide smile.

"My Prince, I don't look good in blue jeans. My belly is too fat," was my initial response. I wasn't lying ... I DO have a gut! I am still about fifty pounds from my goal weight and after losing two hundred pounds from weight loss surgery, I also have folds of loose skin that hangs from my body. I love the girdles that keep it all together under a nicely, flowing dress. The thought of squeezing all of that into a pair of pants makes me cringe.

"Just try them on, Baby, and let me see how you look," he insisted.

Dutifully, I headed to the bedroom, grumbling under my breath like the *Huxtable Mama*. He followed me and watched with Christmas morning glee in his eyes as I pulled the offensive garment up over my thighs and struggled to zip them.

"Here, lemme help you, Baby!" he cried, jumping up to volunteer.

"No, Honey, they are too small. Let's give them to someone else," I insisted as I attempted to remove them.

"Just give me a minute, Baby!" he said as he zipped those jeans on me like they were made for me ... or somebody that looked like me. "Look at my baby!" he beamed with pride while smiling and drooling and looking me up and down. "Your belly may be fat, but your butt is PERFECT!" he said as his eyes softened and that Grinch smile crept across his face.

Needless to say, the jeans didn't remain on me for very long as they ended up on the floor, along with the rest of my clothing.

Compromise is important for friendships and love affairs. My hubby likes to see me wearing pants. In the five years since we have been together, I have added a few pairs of yoga pants and some sweat pants to my wardrobe. I now have t-shirts to wear with my pants, and I recently bought a belt! My granddaddy is still turning over in his grave whenever I squeeze into a pair of blue jeans, but I think he smiles with approval over the pleasure it brings to my Prince. Lord, I thank you for teaching me to compromise, and I thank you for denim!

Bartee Chimes In

"First of all," Bartee begins, "my wife's granddaddy's era was in 1920-something. Times have changed since then (concerning clothing)! Blue jeans are an everyday wear.

If you get 'em dirty, who cares?

If you get holes in 'em, who cares?" (LOL)

Bartee once told me that he believes that blue jeans hold in a lot of unwanted and unneeded fat in place. "Oh! I see! Now, maybe I understand," I responded. "And you don't have to be poor to wear jeans!" he states. I can agree with that statement! Have you seen the price of a pair of blue jeans, these days?

Bartee Continues With

As I said earlier, you can wear blue jeans and get them dirty, have holes in them, and NOBODY CARES, because they are blue jeans! You can go to the park, sit on a bench that is half-way clean ... you can go in a restaurant, slide over on the bench, get some food on the bottom (or the side, or the top), and you can go to church with a nice crease down the middle (with a shirt and a tie). People will look at you and say, "Ooohh, he look good! He must be military!" *(talking 'bout that crease in the middle of your pants)* Put on some blue jeans, some white tennis shoes (clean, that is) or some sandals; and you can wear ANY shirt … Man, that's my style!

**AND THAT GOES FOR BLUE JEAN SHORTS, TOO!!!
LOL**

**Photo credit:
The Anointed Lesley Reed**

CHAPTER 3
HELP ME

I experienced my first anxiety attack in 2006. I didn't know what it was while I was having it. I couldn't breathe, so at first, I thought that what I was feeling was an asthma attack. I began to sweat profusely, and my head was throbbing, but I was in an air-conditioned building! *What was going on with me? What was happening to me?*

After the loss of my job and three suicide attempts, I received a diagnosis of "generalized anxiety disorder and major depression"; I began the process of recognizing those symptoms and learning to live with them. I needed help back then and continue to need it now. Back then, I needed help remembering to take my medication, eating, and bathing. Today, I need help maintaining stress, remembering to eat on time, and trying to stay focused. This sometimes means that I get lost while I am driving.

Bartee wonders, "How do you get lost, driving?" He claims to have never seen me get lost while I am driving. That's because, when I don't know where we are going, I sit in the passenger seat and let HIM drive. Bartee never drives to the same destination, the same route. He can find fifteen different ways to get to the corner store. Me? I prefer the same route each time I go. That way, I don't have to pay attention to where I am going; I only have to pay attention to the other drivers on the road.

Bartee always advises me to pay attention to my surroundings "and everything else that follows." I think I will take his advice - - tomorrow.

"Hey, Baby, will you take my clothes to the cleaners for me?" Bartee asked one morning as he was headed out to work."

"What's the address?" was my response because I knew my trusty GPS would get me there in no time.

"You know the one I'm talking about, Baby. It's down on Whatcha-ma-call-it Street," was his response. Although I had now lived in Daytona Beach with my husband for about three years, I still needed help remembering where landmarks and locations were and how to get from Point A to Point B. Every time we had driven to the dry cleaners in the past, my husband drove to each destination while I checked my phone notifications. Now, he was asking me to go somewhere, and I was sure that I was going to get lost.

"Will you help me?" I asked Bartee.

"Baby, you need to pay attention to where you are going, and where you have been. One day, I might not be here," my loving husband has always said.

My response is always a difficult one to articulate. I love him, because he cares about me, and I am grateful that God blessed Bartee to have the gifts and talents that I need to learn. It is frightening to think about driving myself around without him. It truly is frightening. Bartee even tells me that it shouldn't be frightening! Just about the time the fright begins to well up inside of me, a voice in my Spirit reminds me:

My help comes from the LORD, who made heaven and earth. Psalm 121:2

I can do all things through him who strengthens me. Philippians 4:13

Thank you, Bartee, and thank you Jesus; I got this!

Bartee's Response

First of all, my wife has been riding around Daytona with me as the driver and also driving around Daytona by herself. I continue to tell my wife, "Just pay attention to the streets, signs, and landmarks as we go by, because Daytona is just one big circle-in-a-square box."

All I can do is keep her in my prayers and pray that she will find her way, because there is nothing I really can do. Yet again, I can give her the names of the street or business, and then, she can put the information into her GPS.

Mental illness is nothing to play around with. I am learning step-by-step how to be more aware of the triggers that may cause my wife to lose direction (no pun intended). BUT, riding in the passenger side, I have never seen my wife get lost, yet. LOL

HELP IS ON THE WAY!

Photo by Lesley Reed

CHAPTER 4
WET, SHINY & BLACK

One morning, Bartee was stepping out of the shower and searching for his towel. As I heard him turn off the shower water, I remembered that there was no towel hanging up for him, and I ran to the laundry room to grab a hot towel from the dryer. As I entered the bathroom to hand him his towel, I marveled over my husband. "Wet, Shiny & Black," I said to myself, with a smile on my lips. Bartee noticed my smile, as he retrieved his towel from my hands. I took a step towards him, wrapped the towel around his waist and placed a soft kiss on his wet lips.

As I turned to leave the bathroom, I remembered Ephesians 3:20 that teaches us that God will give us more than we could ask Him for, more than we can imagine, and more than we can ever think of. God certainly did that, for me, when He sent Bartee into my life. Bartee is a man. A man that will burp, fart and has stinky feet. He is also a man that holds me when I cry.

He straightens me when I am crooked, and he prays for my whole body, when only my toe hurts. God made Bartee for me – a man with questions, concerns and opinions. Bartee is a man that can piss me off and make me swoon. Bartee's limitations are masked by my abilities, and his anointed exceptions help to cover my shortfalls.

God loves me enough to send me a man that will alter his habits, just to make me feel comfortable. I remember, on one of our very first out-of-town dates, Bartee said that he was thirsty, and stopped at a convenience store. I waited in the car. He returned to the car, carrying a brown paper bag. He handed me the bottle of water that I had requested, and he proceeded to open a bottle of beer that had emerged from the bag. Now, on this particular occasion, Bartee was driving us to an event. As he lifted the bottle of beer to his lips, I guess he noticed the frown on my face and asked, "What's wrong with you?" My response was, "You don't plan to drive me around with beer on your lips, do you?" A heated discussion ensued; something about him being thirsty and me offering him the bottle of water that was in my hand. As I reminded him of the drinking and driving laws in our state, I also reminded him that he was driving precious cargo in his car ... ME!

Bartee Interjects

"Well, I remember ... well, I don't remember going to an event," Bartee reflects. "I think we were coming back from somewhere, headed home." (I wouldn't have drunk nothing, going to no event.)

"Well, anyway, I threw the beer away, and we never had that conversation again because I understood where she was coming from; and I thank God for placing such a woman in my life with purpose and direction."

I Conclude With

"AWWWW" I love my husband! Sometimes, I truly believe that he "gets" me! He hears my thoughts and my fears, and he considers them! He isn't so quick to say "I got this" or "let me handle this." He actually shows me that he loves me by listening, considering what I say, and applying my thoughts into our reality. Oh my ...

Bartee says: "S-o-m-e-t-i-m-e-s."

Yup ... he is a handful.

Bartee Adds

I am a reaction-type person, and sometimes, I have to tell my wife, "I got this!" so she won't keep giving me A-B-C-D-E-F-G ... when I understood it at A-B-C! Thank you! My wife is sensitive AND needy. (Even her therapist told her that!) Sometimes, they appear at the same time, but I am learning to appreciate the power of prayer! (LOL)

Photo Credit by:

Jhonn De La Puente

Captured at the

2018 Bold Beautiful & Bald Beauty Bazaar

www.BoldBeautifulAndBald.com

www.Facebook.com/BoldBeautifulAndBaldBeautyBazaar

Solomon's Song of Songs

Let him kiss me with the kisses of his mouth—for your love is more delightful than wine.

Song of Solomon 1:2 NLT

God loves Bartee enough to send him a woman that LOVES shiny things! I love twinkling Christmas lights! I love shiny, dangling earrings. I enjoy big rings and bracelets, and I REALLY enjoy a glittery headpiece on my bald head. Bartee enjoys shopping at thrift stores, and his first stop at every store is the jewelry counter. Oh, my! This man has blessed me with so many shiny accessories that I needed a larger jewelry box to hold them all!

Your cheeks are beautiful with earrings,
your neck with strings of jewels.
We will make you earrings of gold,
studded with silver.

Song of Solomon 1:10-11 NLT

"But listen! Although I buy my wife costume jewelry for her stage presence, she has plenty of real gold and diamonds to wear," Bartee proudly proclaims. There are times when we are preparing to leave the house, and I will put on some jewelry. Bartee will say, "Wear your real stuff." "But, Honey, this matches my dress!" I respond. "Wear Your Real Stuff," he says. I always comply. Well, sometimes I do.

Bartee Continues With

YEAH! Sometimes she does, and sometimes she don't!

But I am sure that's how they do it in Hollywood; you wouldn't want to wear your expensive stuff on stage. Who knows what might happen? I DO find some very nice pieces of old sparkling and shining pieces of jewelry that enhance my wife's outfit.

CHAPTER 5
PEACHES & CREAM

~

"THERE'S A RETIRED MAN IN MY BED!"

Everybody said that an adjustment period would be required after Bartee retired. I prayed over the situation and asked God for guidance. God was silent in my ear. "God, should I do anything to prepare for this change in our lives?" God said nothing. I soon realized that I would have to readjust "around" Bartee, as he discovered his new normal.

"Honey, do you want some breakfast before you run out the door?" I asked Bartee.

"Naw," he responded. "I'll get something when I get home."

Six hours later, my husband returns home, looking dehydrated and drained. He was so excited to head out and visit all of his thrift stores that he didn't drink anything, he didn't eat anything, and he didn't take his prescribed medication. This was the day before his scheduled medical checkup. There was a noticeable change in his medical result, because of the untimely consumption of his meds.

"Bartee, let's create a schedule where we can eat on time and take our meds on time. How does that sound?" My husband thought about what I suggested, and he seemed to comply with my suggestions. What I realized is that God didn't need to direct me on this new aspect of our lives ... He simply waited for us to work it out on our own.

Bartee Says

I don't remember spending ALL day at the thrift store, and it don't take long for me to find what I am looking for! My only adjustment for time is that I have A LOT MORE OF IT! LOL!

"Free at last, Free at last!" Now adjusting to my wife's schedule might become a problem. "Honey?" she asks every time I leave. "Do you have your phone?"

"Honey?" she asks. "Did you get some love from your wife?" (She wants a kiss.)

"Honey?" she asks. "Can you turn down the TV a little? I just got one little paragraph to finish typing."

"Honey?" she asks. "Can you come look at this flyer to see if it is ok?"

"Can you come look at this commercial?"

"Can you come listen to this and look at that?"

What did she do BEFORE I retired? LOL

Oh, I know! She would email me ALLLLL of the above and ask me the same question!

"Honey, what do you think of this or that" ... so now, I feel right at home.

Photo by Lesley Reed

CHAPTER 6
THE DANNY CHRONICLES

Bartee has lived, worked, and played in the Volusia County/Central Florida area for quite some time now. He has friends that have participated in his concerts, and he has friends that have helped participate in his decorative lifestyle. Danny is Bartee's friend that can repair, redesign, and decorate a home. Bartee had not been retired more than a month before Danny began coming over to the house to make changes.

Bartee had lived in this home for over five years before I moved into the home in 2013. Bartee is a BIT territorial about our home. He does the decorating; he is a MASTER cleaner; and he knows what works in a home. Most women/wives would probably want to help make decisions on the colors of the furniture, the placement of the wall hangings, and the landscaping ideas. In fact, we have agreed that HE will do the decorating, and I will just help keep our home clean (LOL!)

Danny has come over to hang our TVs on the walls of our home. I now have new sinks and mirrors and electrical outlets in our home. I may not have any input in these new changes in our home, but I certainly appreciate my husband and his talented buddy Danny for the new upgrades to our home.

Then, the time came for us to paint the outside of the house. We had received a couple of "friendly reminder" letters from the Home Owner's Association concerning the stains and faded paint on our home, and I even saved up a little "piece of change" to help pay for it!

"Bartee, what color can we paint the house?" I had asked for the umpteenth time.

"I got this, Baby! I am gonna paint the house when I am ready to paint!" he said.

Bartee's Point of View

Now that I have retired, the house is painted! "How Ya Like Me Now?"

My wife had me drive her around the neighborhood for some exterior color suggestions. We both agreed to a white house with tan trim. Boy, I am SO happy that it's done! And that's not the only problem! Now, she keeps asking me about painting the INSIDE of the house! SMH.

I'm only human; don't ask me for too much, too fast.

Sitting on Grandma's porch
Detroit, Circa August 2018

CHAPTER 7
COVID-19 CONFINEMENT CHRONICLES

～

As the global pandemic began to grow, and U.S. citizens were encouraged to stay indoors, Bartee began his home improvement projects, and I began to write. I had so much in my head to write, that I soaked off my acrylics, filed my fingernails to a stub, and began to bang out chapters on my keyboard. It was exhilarating! The following short stories were originally posted on my Facebook timeline during the confinement period. They were just too good to leave there, so now I am sharing them with you. I affectionately refer to them as

"Tales from Our Confinement – COVID-19 Stories"

– Angie BEE

www.Facebook.com/ConfinementChroniclesByAngieB
EEproductions

"Where Is My CD?"

Bartee had been searching for this one particular CD since February 29th (the day of Jasmine and Eric's wedding). At first, he thought that he had left this CD in the car because we had sent the kids off on their honeymoon in the car.

"I bet they were jamming to my CD during their entire trip," he proudly proclaimed.

"No dear, they don't jam to your old school music. Kids today have their OWN music to jam to," I told him.

"Hmmph," was his reply. "That's a good CD. They betta recognize!" SMH

So, the kids returned from their honeymoon along with the car. The CD ain't in the car.

"Hey Eric! do you have my CD in your car?" my husband asks.

I whisper to him, "The kids ain't got no CD player in their car, Honey. Kids today listen to music on their phones." "No, Sir. We don't have it, haven't seen it," is my new son's response. #iLoveMeSomeHim

"Hmmph ... where is my CD? That's a good CD! I need to find my CD. I bet Jasmine has it." (Lord, help ... if Eric ain't got it ... I can guarantee that Jasmine ain't got it!)

Bartee searches high and low for this one particular CD. I can't help him look for it because I don't even know what the name of the CD is (you know how that goes). He searches both cars, the back porch music collection, under the seats of both cars and both trunks.

"Where is my CD?" he wonders. "I betcha Jasmine gave it to Angelyn, and now Chris is jamming to my music!" he proclaims.

"CAN I JUST BUY YOU ANOTHER FRICKING CD?!!!"

I scream in frustration.

#ExcuseMyLanguageLord #WashMyMouthOutWithSoap

Bartee has the outside of the house painted. – No CD

Bartee lays new, lovely white rocks in the landscaping in the front of the house. – No CD

Bartee violates confinement – he is older than 65 years of age – and goes to the store, to shop for nothing that we need. – No CD

Bartee comes home last night and says to me, "They closed the Goodwill, Baby. It's bad out there."

#MyPoorHusband

– No CD

#LetUsPray

This morning, he finally decides to unpack his suitcase and his music collection bag from the wedding. Bartee provided music for the wedding and reception, so he had an entire bag of music that he had packed—"just in case." As soon as he unzips the bag of music, I hear him proclaim, "HERE IS MY CD!"

Praise the LORD, this man has found his CD! I am shouting hallelujah and speaking in tongues! GOD IS GOOD!

He pops the CD in the player in our living room, and then proceeds to leave the house! #DontYouWannaListenToIt ?

"Imma go find some new ceiling fans to install. I'll be back, Baby!" Then, I watch him drive off, in his car, while the CD is playing in the house.

So now, I am writing chapters for this next book, and I am jamming to his CD.

It IS a good CD!

#AngieBEEandBarteeProductions
#iLoveMyHusbandAndHeLovesMe
#COVID19 #ConfinementChronicles

"Did I Do That?"

My morning glory! Father, I thank you for the following blessings in my life:

1. We enjoyed an early afternoon drive in the car. When we stopped at the red light, and the motorcyclist next to us coughed, we brought our butts back home.

#Quarantine #COVID19

2. While chilling on the couch, I was enjoying time, playing with my phone. (Father, I should have read the instruction manual.)

#LackOfKnowledge
#EnlargeMyTerritory

3. Suddenly, Bartee's phone started beeping. He was receiving several text messages from my phone, but I didn't send them!

#Jesus #GimmeAclue #StoryGetsWorse

#BeforeItGetsBetter

4. Next thing I know, Angelyn Chestang has "dropped in" on my Alexa!

#MommaAreYouOk?
#ImChillingOnTheCouch
#SomethingWrongWithBarteesPhone
#WhyYouCallingMeOnAlexa?

5. Angelyn then says, "I received an emergency text from you, mom. It included this picture of your ceiling fan!" #OhMy #DidIdoThat?

6. Then, my Facebook Messenger is ringing! My

#1Favorite BlueEyedSon Chris Swansburg is calling. "Ma! I'm putting on my pants, I've got my gun, and I'm headed your way! Just hold on!"

#Huh?

#YouWantMeToFrySomeChicken?

#DoYouNeedMoney?

#YouAreAlwaysWelcome
#ButWhyYouComingOver?

7. So, I ask Angelyn (who is still talking to me through my Alexa), Alexa ... uh, Angelyn, why is Chris coming over?

#Lord #ImSoConfused
#BarteesPhoneIsStillBeeping

#NowIneedToPee

8. Ma! Your text message sent us a locator map, an audio recording, and a message that said "HELP ME!" It went to your emergency contacts!

#OhMy #OhNo #LordHelp #WhereAreMyGlasses?

#IhaveEmergencyContacts?

#WhoKnew?

9. Bartee woke up to find out what the commotion was. "Chris, take off your pants, and put your gun away. I'm ok and I'm sorry about that text. I was playing with my phone. I don't even know how that happened. Besides, I've got no chicken to fry."

#HeLovesHisMama
#HeWasAlreadyInHisCar
#HeStoppedAtKFC

10. Finally, Jasmine called. "Mommy, are you ok?" Her voice sounded sad and shaken. Even though Angelyn had messaged her that this was a false alarm, my youngest still wanted to hear my voice.

#God

#IamGratefulForHumor
#IamGratefulForKidsThatCare
#ConfinementLeadsToDiscovery
#ThankYou #Jesus

Bartee Interjects

"You ain't add what I said during all of this!"

What did you say, dear?

"I said to Alexa, Angelyn, Chris AND Jasmine … I GOT THIS!"

Bartee continues with, "Nobody asked how I was?!" LOL

Yup, Bartee got this and he got ME, 2.

Taken at Cousin Chris's 70's Birthday Party

Detroit Michigan, Circa 2019

I'm a Cheap Date

Our first date was over dinner at Red Lobster. In our first book, I revealed that Bartee had waited patiently for me to finish a meeting with the Christian rappers, following an outdoor concert. The rappers had been bickering, my tummy was growling, and my mind was wondering if "the little Chocolate Man would wait for me" after the meeting.

Praise the Lord! Bartee was waiting for me in the church sanctuary when I emerged from the meeting. He asked me, "What are you going to do, now?" My reply had something to do with my growling tummy, and his reply brought a smile upon my face. I found myself in the passenger seat of his car, headed to eat those yummy cheddar biscuits!

As the result of having gastric bypass surgery in 2011, I don't eat a full restaurant adult serving. The kiddie menu is less than appetizing, so I tend to need a to-go box for my leftovers. In my mind, this makes me a "cheap date", because my leftovers make a GREAT lunch for the next day! During our past seven years together, my cooking skills have not improved, and Bartee's appetite has not decreased, so we generally eat out at restaurants three or four times a week. This means our refrigerator is FULL of to-go boxes. I am still a cheap date!

"Honey, what do you want for dinner?" I frequently ask my hubby.

"Oh, I dunno," is his inevitable reply. Once I begin to pull out the numerous leftovers, the jokes begin.

"Well, you can make meatloaf from the so-and-so restaurant. Or, you can have chicken from the such-and-such restaurant."

"Naw, let's just go out to eat."

I return the leftovers to the refrigerator and gleefully hop in the passenger seat of his car.

I don't ask for much. I don't mind eating leftovers; I will wear last season's dresses. I pay for my own nails, and I ditched the expensive wigs! I am a cheap date! As long as I am with my hubby, the blessing of love that I get from him is certainly sweeter than any material item I could ever crave.

Bartee Says

First of all, ... I started to leave the church sanctuary because the meeting was taking TOO long! But, in the nick of time, Angela emerged. Now, she had just left the meeting, and she was still sitting around talking! So, after she said goodbye to her tour members, and her friends at the church, and everybody else ... her good-byes weren't as long as the meeting, but when an evangelist is leaving the building, they take a LONG time saying goodbye! ... we started OUR conversation and then decided to go out to get something to eat.

Now that we are married, we eat out a lot! My wife doesn't eat a lot, so we always have food "To-Go." She sometimes tries to eat food off my plate. Sometimes, she has asked to share a meal, so we wouldn't have to bring food home. BUT I always say, "NO." (Well, I don't always say NO, but the majority of time I do because I want to eat ALL OF MY FOOD THAT I ORDERED!

I'm selfish like that!

Light, in the Midst of Darkness

1. My hubby loves to watch Cuomo on CNN. Before he retired, he would try to stay up late enough to watch the news, but he would generally fall asleep on the couch, instead. Now that he sleeps in later, he can stay up later! Just the other night, he was absolutely fascinated watching Cuomo interview the Governor of New York.

#Lord #IappreciateHumor #ThisIsAgoodOne #IwasLaughingWhileIwasTyping

2. "Hey, Baby!" Bartee says. "These two remind me of each other. They talk alike!" My sleepy husband proclaims from the couch.

#Jesus #KeepMyFaceStraight

3. "Well, dear," I reply, "they are both from New York, and they are both Italian." I giggle from the next room. #Father #KeepMyPeace #IknowHeIsSleepy #TryingTo StayUpLate

#WatchingCuomoInterviewCuomo

4. "No, really, Baby!" he exclaims. "The more I look at them, they even look alike! You need to come in here and see this!"

#God #iLoveMyHusbandAndHeLovesMe and I need to get this man to bed at a reasonable hour. I KNOW that

He knows why they look and sound alike ... but the #confinement and the #LateNights are getting to him.

5. "Honey, I think they both grew up in the same town. Maybe even in the same family. What are their names, again?" I ask him, shouting from the bedroom, trying to keep a straight face

#Jesus #YouAnsweredMyPrayers from #2

6. The quiet that comes next is something that I will not soon forget. The voices from the TV were the only sound you could hear, echoing through our home. Bartee didn't make a move on the leather couch. He didn't make a sound. He wasn't slurping from his cup, and he wasn't chomping on his favorite pistachios. He was just quiet!

Maybe he had finally fallen asleep? Maybe something else was happening. I had to go and investigate for myself. As I rose from my massaging, adjustable bed that Jasmine Elyse Simmons got for us, and I put down the pink water jug that Ricky Rey gave me, I slid into my ultra-comfy slippers that Chris Swansburg and Angelyn Chestang gave me for Christmas, and I headed for the bedroom door, to check on my hubby.

#MyFamily #MyBabies #TheirLoveSurroundsMe #Iam AspoiledMom

7. "BABY!!!!" my fascinated hubby yells!

#MyPoorNeighbors #IknowTheyCanHearHim
#AdeafManCouldHearThatExcitement #DidGodFinally
OpenHisEyes

"They are talking about their mom and spaghetti! They are BROTHERS! He called him a MEATBALL!" The grin on Bartee's face was truly delightful as the revelation appeared on his face, and he continued to watch TV. Have you ever seen a small child's face light up when you give them a toy or a piece of candy? That is what my husband's face looked like!

#PURE #Joy

8. PRAISE THE LORD FOR SLEEPY REVELATION! My husband, the King of our Castle and the Prince of my Heart, finally woke up long enough to realize that the Cuomos are brothers!

#MrSmithWasntInterviewingMrJones #Cuomo #Really?

9. As I composed this post, I kept hearing the voice of God say, "Light in the Darkness."

Father, thank you for the joy of humor and the ability to laugh at one another. Thank you for clarity and peace of mind. Lord, thank you for blessing our hearts and minds to hear from you, and thank you for the ability to see the joy in the midst of this pandemic darkness. I appreciate my sister MzFran Cash for being a TRUE light in my life. I'm gonna call her today, just to let her know that! #LoveYouSis

Thank you for 2 Corinthians 4:6 which says, *For God, who said, "Let light shine out of darkness," has shone in our hearts to give the light of the knowledge of the glory of God in the face of Jesus Christ."* (ESV)

10. Father, I pray for Albany, GA, and all those dealing with #Covid19 in the city where my daughter Angelyn Chestang was born. I ask that you comfort Sonya Bennett and all those in my childhood home of Detroit that are trying to manage; some are even confined at home, alone. Please keep my daughters safe as they continue to go back and forth to work, and please anoint our community leaders to hear from you, and act on YOUR words. Thank you for pain, as it helps to keep me focused on your grace, healing, and your love. Finally, thank you for the #Cuomo #Brothers and their entire family. For us, they were a light, in the midst of this darkness. Bless them indeed, and Thank you! Thank you! Thank you! Amen

Bartee Adds

First of all, I stay up every night – before and after I retired. I watched the news until 11:30 PM. This was the first time that I have seen Chris Cuomo interview his brother; or known that he even HAD a brother to interview! Once I started listening to the voices, it finally connected! Both brothers (in my opinion) are very knowledgeable of the inner-workings of Washington, D.C., and have strong family values.

Angie BEE Concludes With

"I hope the Cuomo Brothers purchase several copies of this book!" LOL!

CHAPTER 8
I DON'T KNOW
WHAT I'M SQUEEZING

B artee lived alone for quite some time before my perky, happy behind moved into his home. Generally speaking, it was a smooth transition, but there are times when I believe that my husband still acts like a "man-alone."

"I can't get the thing to get in there, baby," I heard my husband say from the garage.

"Come on now, baby, get up there!" he said on another day from the laundry room.

"Baby, I don't know what I'm squeezing!" was his comment just yesterday while he was working on our brand-new Epson printer.

During each comment, I was generally in the other room. In each case, I replied to his comment with, "Are you talking to me, Honey?"

"Naw, Baby! I'm talking to myself / I'm talking to this whatcha-ma-call-it" would be his reply.

"Well, I respond when you call me Baby. If you gonna start calling OTHER stuff Baby, I ain't gonna respond," was my response!

"Damn it, baby!" my hubby said.

I KNOW you ain't talking to me, now! Hmmph!

Sometimes, when we are accustomed to doing things one way, we must adjust to accommodate others when they enter our lives. For example, when we bring a new puppy into the home, we must adjust to feed, care for, and walk that new pet. If we are accustomed to talking to ourselves in an empty home and someone new moves into the home, we need to adjust to that new set of ears in the home. How have Bartee and I managed to adjust to this situation?

I have managed to adjust to this situation by ignoring Bartee's voice, when he is in another room talking!

Sometimes he may be on the phone with one of his buddies. He ain't talking to me, so I go on with whatever I was doing.

"Hey, Baby! What we got on the calendar next Wednesday?" he yells from the living room.

"Are you talking to me?" is generally my reply.

"Well, I sure as hell ain't calling *Charlie* my Baby!" is his sarcastic response.

Oh no, did he try to get smart with me? He must have forgotten who he is talking to!

So, on this day, I decide to wake up and "try a little tenderness" with my husband. I realized that Colossians 4:6 says that my *"words should be seasoned with salt"*, and since I love salt, I figured I could ACE this conversation! "Bartee?" I began, composing in my mind. I imagined that my voice would be with as much love and submission that I could compile. "Honey? How about we start something new when we are together? How about, if you are NOT talking to me, you keep your comments in your head, or you whisper them to yourself. That way, when I actually DO hear your voice, I know that you are talking to me. What do you think of that?"

I am still waiting to have this actual conversation with Bartee.

Let your conversation be always full of grace, seasoned with salt, so that you

may know how to answer everyone.

Colossians 4:6 NIV

Bartee's Response

My wife's name is Angela.

If I needed to speak to her, I would say "Angela, da-da-da-da-da."

Now, she just assumes that when I am talking to myself out loud, that I am talking to her. If I need to address my wife or ask a question, I know how to say "Angela" and then finish what I need to ask or say. My wife needs to understand it's not all about her. I talk to myself; I answer myself; and I am okay with that!

**Captured after our mental health workshop
Atlanta Georgia, April 2018**

CHAPTER 9
WHEN THE MUSIC DON'T MATCH THE GROOVE

～

As a family, friends, and followers all know, I am Da Queen Bee of Holy Hip Hop music. I hosted a radio show for over a decade that featured Christian Rap music. I interviewed recording artists and was the MC for dozens of concerts. Kids gave their lives to Christ during our tour stops, and these years of servitude led to my ordination as an Evangelist.

Our family, friends, and followers also know that Bartee is known as the Rage of the Stage with his Smooth Jazz, R&B and Vintage Soul concerts. His vocals will make you appreciate Motown music lyrics, and his infectious stage presence will make even grandma get up and boogie! Bartee has performed for decades, and he truly believes that God has anointed him in this capacity. Many people have asked him, "Why don't you sing gospel music?" His response is always, "That is not what God equipped me to do"; I agree with that.

In our home, the music has a bit of a different feel.

"Alexa, play my favorite radio station," I instruct our Echo Dot that sits on our kitchen island. Instantly, I hear music from Flame, Lecrae, Da Truth, KB and even Snoop Dog. I love the volume that I get from that little round dot, and I love the inspiration that I feel from the lyrics that accompany the beat. Bartee, on the other hand, is not really up to speed on the latest in Christian rap.

"Who is that? Eminem?" my husband asks.

"Nope, that's Andy Mineo," is my reply.

"Which one is that?" he asks.

"That is Tedashi."

"Did you hear that line when he said ..." my voice trails off into oblivion as I realize my husband has exited the kitchen and has escaped. He really is a singer and a lover of songs. He only tolerates rap when he has to.

"Alexa, STOP," is my command as I hear the garage door close. It's time for DJ Angie BEE to switch up from the rap music to the soul music. My husband has returned from his shopping excursion at The Goodwill, and I try to make the home inviting for him, when he returns.

"Play music from Bill Withers," I command the Echo Dot. As Bartee lingers in the garage (probably hiding his purchases from me), the next song that echoes through the dot is a song about a war-time soldier that got shot in his shoulder. This soldier can't write a letter because he isn't left-handed. He asks that someone write a letter to his mother and the preacher. He even has pity and forgiveness for the Vietnamese solder that shot him! OH, MY WORD! Where did THESE lyrics come from? By the time Bartee emerges from the garage and into the kitchen where I am standing, I am a blubbering, tearful mess!

"Who writes this stuff? This is so sad!" I proclaim, as I fling myself into my husband's confused arms.

"What happened? When I left the house, you were bopping and praising God. When I come home, you're crying to war songs!" he asks me.

Sometimes, I try to experience the presence of God in the music that my husband loves. On this day, Bill Withers brought me right to the steps of the Most Holy.

Bartee Says

My wife is SO sensitive AND needy! Sensitivity can be a good thing that the world needs more of. Sometimes, my wife gets in to *The Twilight Zone* where she seems to cry with empathy for life's underdog, which is good ... don't get me wrong, but sometimes, she has to put on her "Big Girl Panties (bloomers, drawers, etc) and understand "It's just a movie."

LOL

Vacationing in Detroit at the Hard Rock Café, before it closed Summer 2018

CHAPTER 10
COLD AND WINDY
LOVE CONQUERS ALL

~

I remember the first time my daughter Jasmine introduced us to her fella Eric. It was during her 25th birthday party. The families all met in Jacksonville near my daughter's home. My parents were in town for their annual vacation, so we were all thrilled to go eat and celebrate. The trunk of my SUV was filled with gifts for Jasmine and plants for her sister Angelyn. (I can't have a party for one daughter, and not give the other daughter a gift, too!)

I couldn't WAIT to meet Eric in person! We had already met on webcam, but I wanted to see his interactions between the families. How did he act around Jasmine's proud-and-particular father? How would he respond to my daddy's stern-but-comforting handshake? What would he say, and how would be respond to my quiet-yet-watchful husband? Yup, this young man was about to go through the ringer!

Eric not only survived the ringer, but two years later, on February 29, 2020, he cried with joy as Jasmine was escorted by her father, to stand by his side. They wed on the beach at Amelia Island, in front of nearly one hundred of their friends and family. The location was PERFECT for them, and it was a loving gathering for the entire family. It was a cold and windy day on that Florida beach that morning, but by the time Jasmine was walking down the aisle, the sun was at its highest point in the sky, and the "son" was beaming on them both.

I was honored to officiate the wedding. I had conducted their pre-marital counseling via Facebook Messenger, and their responses are the stuff that love stories are made of. Bartee and I are encouraging them to write their true love story like we did. We shall see what happens. It is a blessing to see two young people find true love, the way God meant it to be. Eric "found" Jasmine while walking past a shopping center where she worked. Bartee "found" me as he drove past a church billboard that announced that my evangelism troupe was coming to town. Men, let the Lord direct your footsteps; women, let the Lord put His responses in your mouth and in your heart. Do these things each and every day and watch LOVE CONQUER ALL because God is love!

Beloved, let us love one another, for love is from God, and whoever loves has been born of God and knows God.

1 John 4:7 ESV

Bartee Says

First of all, for me, meeting parents and relatives or friends and family, I am a little different. I'm glad that Eric responded well to his interrogation. When I find someone that I am interested in —now this is ME talking — I'm interested in that person and not particularly her family OR friends. If we choose to connect to one another, and if we choose to love one another, I would pray for God's blessing. Sometimes, family and friends can be your downfall if you let them in too deep into your life. Be steadfast in your life, cling close to God, and remember "What God has Put Together, Let no Man OR Woman, Child, Friend, Family ..." you know the rest.

CHAPTER 11
A SUPERHERO
IN MY BEDROOM

I am not going to lie. We got married on August 9, 2013, and I didn't "come up for air" until August 15th. Bartee was getting the job done, and I was shouting out the name of Our Lord.

(Oh Jesus! Yes, Lord!)

I guess there is a certain sexual freedom when you are older, kids are grown, bills are paid, and there is no chance of you getting pregnant.

(Yes, Lord! Oh, right there! You got it, now!)

It seemed like through the good, the bad, and the learning curves of our relationship, Bartee was always a simple man with simple desires and expectations. He wasn't looking for me to wear a thong during the day, or a negligee to bed at night (THANK GOD). He didn't expect burning candles or romantic music at our bedside, and he didn't even care if I had showered or not (LOL)! He is just a simple man that loves me, and he knows that I love him. Our lovemaking is EPIC, and I praise God for it, each and every time it happens.

So then, the bedroom TV goes out.

It happened during the pandemic, so we REALLY needed to replace it before the world ended. I mean, we got our adjustable, vibrating bed just for lovemaking and WATCHING TV!

"Let me go to that store and find another Open Box TV", my beloved husband proclaimed. "No, My Prince; the store is closed due to the pandemic. You gotta shop online," I declared. After two hours of scrolling and comparing prices, I picked one that I thought would be GREAT for us! "We don't need no smart TV in the bedroom" was his response.

Hmmmph…. He just don't know, do he?

Bartee's Response

First of all, *I don't like no smelly woman*! So, I DO CARE how my wife comes to bed, or even how she maintains her hygiene. BUT! Give me some smooth jazz music to set the scene, and that's all she wrote!

I am a simple man with simple pleasures. No freaky stuff, please!

CHAPTER 12
HE AIN'T OLD;
HE'S MY LOVER

———————— ∿ ————————

When you marry a man that is eleven years your senior, you begin to notice that there are certain sayings that really make you wonder. Such as the expressions:

"They talked about Jesus!" – What the hell does that mean?

"God Rest the Dead" – Huh?

"Lord willing, and the creek don't rise" – Say again?

"The Icebox is Cold" – What the ... ?!

Bartee Says

Keep living! You will hear a lot more of sayings coming from my past. Some of what I say is original, and some is not.

Collaboration and Submission May Lead to Elevation

Originally written and published in

RISE Magazine

By "Da Queen Bee" Angie BEE

Well, you are now an entrepreneur, and you are operating your own business, making your own decisions and calling your own shots. It's kind of exciting, isn't it? You feel blessed and invigorated and sometimes, even a bit challenged. If you came from a corporate job prior to launching your endeavor, you may have become accustomed to receiving a regular paycheck with possible benefits, surrounded by a regular schedule. Now, your income is a direct result of your productivity, accounts receivable dependability, and your own marketing and advertising budget. You may or may not have a staff and inventory concerns; so how do you elevate and grow personally or professionally when you have all of this responsibility on your shoulders?

How do you elevate your company when you are struggling to keep your head above water? How do you increase your income, sustain your employees and remain motivated when productivity can lapse if you take a day off work? Why should you support fellow entrepreneurs when you need funds to increase visibility? Some entrepreneurs even consider returning to that corporate job part time as an option to generate much-needed revenue.

Consider a collaboration to help to reach your business goals! Working with other entrepreneurs may not only increase your product and service lines, but can also be affordable. Think about bartering with a business that would complement yours. For example, a florist could collaborate with a local caterer. Each business could promote the services of the other so that clients may receive flowers, food, and quality service at an affordable rate Collaboration may lead to elevation!

The Bible tells us in the 1st book of Peter, Chapter 5, verse 6, *Therefore humble yourselves under the mighty hand of God, that He may exalt you at the proper time*. Now what does that mean? Some people consider a humble nature in the business world as a target-for-a-takeover! On the other-hand, an aggressive businesswoman is sometimes referred to by "less-than-favorable" terms, as our efforts may be intimidating to others. Even more frequently, a spiritual businessperson may be considered weak and unable to make harsh decisions as "*they* are *led by God*" in their personal actions and their business deeds. The Christian businessperson may be more "generous" with their giving than others, as their company grows. Joyce Meyer once shared a story of a former accountant that she employed. This person told Joyce that she "gave too much money to the church" and that it was "not advised" for her to do so. Meyer responded by verbally rejecting that idea, and she continues to be a generous and joyful giver. If this scripture tells us that we may be "exalted" if we humble ourselves, how do we help the non-believers that are in business for themselves?

Submission may lead to elevation!

"How?" you may ask. "Why?" you may ask. How do I submit to someone else when I am the boss? Why should I submit to something else when I am in charge? Let us look at the success of certain structures to inspire and inform us on this topic.

Within the hierarchy of a "successful" family, you have a leader (a father), an anchor (a mother) some pets (enjoyable contributions to a family), and maybe some children (your reason for waking each morning). Each aspect of the family pulls their own weight and contributes to the success of the family, and each family member has their own way of draining the family, as well. The pets must submit or be punished. The kids must learn and submit; and the Bible teaches us that wives should submit to their husbands.

Now, look at a corporate structure. There are employees, managers, executives, and in some cases, a deciding Board of Directors. We have been educated to learn about this hierarchy, and in most cases, we DO submit to authority. Now, if we learned to submit in our family structure, and we receive compensation as the result of our submission in the corporate world, why do we not submit as entrepreneurs? Why do we not read, study, and submit to the word of God as our instruction for elevation?

Collaboration is a form of submission where each collaborator compromises to make the collaboration successful for both parties. Submission is also a form of collaboration where you learn to follow instructions, obey the rules, and receive a reward for your efforts!

We all want to rise in our efforts. Some of us strive to make others proud of our efforts, and others are simply trying to make a living by using the gifts and talents they are blessed to have. Do not go it alone! Find someone to collaborate with, and learn from someone that you can submit to – like a mentor! Read the Bible, and apply what you have learned from it to your life, and your business, and get ready ... your elevation will come in the proper time!

Faithfully submitted by

Evangelist Angie BEE

www.DaQueenBee.com

For more inspirational messages, I invite you to come LIKE my page at

www.facebook.com/DaQueenBeeEvangelistAngieBEE

ABOUT EVANGELIST ANGIE BEE

In April 2010, Angie BEE was diagnosed with major depression and generalized anxiety disorder, immediately following her second of three suicide attempts. Years later, as she faithfully entered her third marriage in 2013, she was further diagnosed with PTSD. Determined to serve the Lord with gladness, Angie BEE launched an evangelism troupe featuring concerts, workshops, and retreats. She wrote three books from 2010 to 2013, and collaborated on three more. She contributed to several blogs and magazine publications online and in print, and even became a health ambassador by working with her husband to launch an annual alopecia awareness health and beauty bazaar. She travels to conduct book signings and speak on mental health awareness events. She preaches from a prophetic and testimonial anointing; she uses her years of experience as a radio show host to narrate and produce audiobooks for other authors. Evangelist Angie

BEE has also been recognized by the following community leaders:

- Community Service Award from Triumphant Magazine

- Curly Girls Hair Festival – Presenter/Speaker Award for Alopecia Awareness

- Literacy Is A Legacy Award from the F.R.E.S.H. Book Festival, Daytona Beach

- The Professional Women of Excellence, Inc., National Chapter President

- Mary & Martha Ministries in Orlando

- Best Female Radio Show Host Recognition from The Global One Accord DJ Alliance

See her past projects at

www.Facebook.com/AngieBEEproductions, secure her books online at www.DaQueenBee.com, and send an email to EvangelistAngieBEE@gmail.com for book signings and speaking engagements.

ABOUT BARTEE

B artee is affectionately referred to as "The Rage of The Stage" and is highly sought after throughout Central Florida. This sensational R&B singer began his career at the age of eleven in his hometown of Akron, Ohio. He continues to share his natural-born feeling for music just as aggressively as he first did decades ago. Always sought after, Bartee is a versatile entertainer that performs Smooth Jazz, a Motown Review showcase, and Vintage Soul.

Bartee has shared the stage with music icons such as James Ingram, Howard Hewitt, The Ohio Players, Linda Cole & The O'Jays. Bartee leads the *Dads-on-Duty* workshop while on *The TOUR that Angie BEE Presents,* and he leads by Angie BEE's side in the *God, Me & You* workshop, as well. You can find Bartee performing a Motown Review concert during *The TOUR* weekend retreats for couples, and he continues to serve the Lord with gladness through his lifestyle and commitment to his family.

In 2013, Bartee met, dated, and married Angie BEE in less than six months. Before he met her, he vowed to NEVER remarry, and she vowed NEVER to submit to another man. God orchestrated something different for the two of them, and this book reveals the details.

Bartee first became a published author on August 1, 2017. As co-author, he and his wife Angie BEE wrote *In the Beginning: There Was God, Me & You* published by Ladero Press. This book reveals their true love story that only God could have written.

Working with his wife, Bartee has contributed stories to the inspiration audiobook collaboration series *Confinement Chronicles.* You may hear his voice, his words, and even a song when you listen! Visit www.Facebook.com/ConfinementChroniclesByAngieBEEproductions to order your copy.

Bartee always wanted to write a book and will soon write his life story of juvenile incarceration to prison, and God's many blessings in his life.

Together, Bartee and Angie BEE have two adult sons and two adult daughters with sons-in-love. Search for Bartee online at www.BarteeSings.com and follow him at www.facebook.com/pg/BarteeTheAuthor